HAPPY AT WORK

Career Yau

CARRIE STRINGHAM

HAPPY AT WORK:
Career Yaw

Copyright © 2023 by Carrie Strigham

Published by:

Paperback ISBN: 979-8-9882844-0-6
Library of Congress Control Number:

Cover Designer: Fusion Creative Works
Interior Book Layout: Fusion Creative Works

Every attempt has been made to properly source all quotes.

Printed in The United States of America

First Edition

2 4 6 8 10 12

CONTENTS

INTRODUCTION

Do you feel satisfaction, peace, and even joy, when you think about what you do every day? If not, you've picked up the right book. You can experience joy in what you do and what you call work, every day. The formula isn't magic. It's available to you right now and I'm going to help you find it. Whether you are a young adult uncertain about what it is you should do with your life, a stay-at-home parent looking to get back into the workforce, or a mid-lifer feeling like you've never found your right work, you can find work that makes you crazy-happy, that brings you joy, and that makes you want to get up in the morning. You don't have to work in a mediocre, means-to-an-end job that makes you feel stuck, depleted, or drained at the end of the day. You have a choice. You can be Happy at Work and experience career movement with meaning.

I wasn't planning on becoming a Career Coach even though I've been doing it in one capacity or another most of my adult life. In my 20s, while working as faculty for a private college, I found myself teaching a course designed to help adults make decisions about a career path, all the while zig-zagging through my own career choices. Often, I was helping a friend make decisions about career direction while coaching employees in their employment choices in my various leadership positions.

In my 30s, I worked for a national healthcare entity. We had a corporate office up north and another corporate office down south. When the two merged, I was able to facilitate career coaching sessions for those employees not wanting to move across the United States and those who did. During most of this time, I worked in academia and in various professions in lead human resource positions. Not only was I assessing internal and external candidate abilities and interests to fill positions in organizations with anywhere from 1,000 to 27,000 employees, but I was working to boost work team performance to help each employee develop their strengths and talents.

As a professor, I found that students would ask me for career direction and advice. Often a student would approach me with a hopeless look on their face and explain that they had been in school for three years, and all this time, they had been working on a degree that didn't really hold any appeal for them. Usually, they wanted to find a way to salvage what they had already completed in the way of coursework. Sometimes there was a way for us to do this. You will read more about how you can do the same later in this book.

The irony in what I was doing as I helped others find their own career directions wasn't lost on me. I've held many positions, partly because of my varied interests and partly because of life changes, including multiple moves across the United States. I finally embraced the fact that my career trajectory, which was anything but a straight line, was part of what made my coaching so useful to others. Here are just a few of the jobs I've had. I've worked for a bonding company (not that kind!), as a bank manager, in healthcare as part of a senior management team, in human resources, in the mining industry, and as a professor. I've worked at a bookstore, at McDonald's, in retail, and as a piano teacher. I've owned four different businesses. I've worked as a K through 12 substitute teacher, as a licensed Optician, and have held so many volunteer positions that to list them all would surely put you to sleep. How could I possibly be qualified to help other people find their professional callings when I had so much change and upheaval on my own career path? And aren't there already more than a few career experts out there? What made and continues to make my approach any different than all the others?

It wasn't until I found myself middle-aged, contemplating yet another career shift as my teenage daughter began struggling with her own career direction, that I realized that I had been living in my right career field all along. It was at the same time I realized that my experiences and my ability to apply what I had learned in one industry or profession to make a shift to yet another, was part of what made my approach unique. My friends, colleagues, and family simply said, "We could have told you this years ago." I'm happy that they didn't. I needed to travel the path of discovery on my own.

Throughout this book, you will read about real people, although I've changed their names and the details in their stories. It was easy for me to find examples of people who were stuck in their jobs or contemplating a career change. I found examples of people who broke away from what they thought they wanted, what they fell into, or what their parents wanted for them, to find jobs that left them feeling more than a little bit high. Some of their stories may resonate with you. Take what fits and discard the rest. Long ago, I learned that if I get just one or two really big ah-ha pieces from something, then I've hit the mother lode. I trust the same will hold true for you.

Getting Stuck

We all get stuck from time to time and need someone or something to help us to move forward. It's human nature. But sometimes we stay stuck. Sometimes, a day turns into a week and a week turns into a month, and soon, a year or more has passed. We might get stuck when we are trying to find our right job, our right work, or our vocational calling; all terms that I use interchangeably throughout this book.

Maybe you are stuck in quicksand. Or maybe you are just needing a little shift. You are likely thinking that you aren't quite ready to quit your job and take a giant leap into the unknown. You don't need to. This book isn't about cliff jumping, although cliff jumping may be just what you need. You will make mistakes, but your work should fit you like your favorite pair of shoes. They might take a few days to break in, but you will know almost immediately that you have found a pair that you want to put on every morning. I want you to realize that your work can feel the same way!

Career Yaw

You are about to embark on an exciting adventure. You are about to experience your work life the way it is meant to be – full, rewarding, uplifting, and adventurous. You are about to move down the career path that is right for you at this point in your life, to experience a Career Yaw.

I have coined the term Career Yaw.

**Yaw is a term that is used to describe an oscillation or a twist, often referring to a moving aircraft or a moving ship. It is a definitive movement off the charted course. In the context of this book, yaw refers to an oscillation or a twist off a charted career path.
It is finding your right work and charting your own course.**

You may experience a Career Yaw multiple times during your work life. Many of you have stories that could be included in this book! Working for decades in the same industry in the same job for the same employer is a thing of the past. There are exceptions, but if you selected this book, we could probably surmise that you are not an exception.

Get ready for a yaw off your current career path! Let's have some fun charting your new course.

Career Calling

People who have found their vocational callings all seem to agree that while life isn't necessarily easier, it sure is more rewarding. We each have a calling. Or maybe several callings depending on where we are in our lives.

Our callings can, and often do, change. Whether you believe we enter this world with a predetermined calling or you believe that we have to find our calling makes no difference. Maybe you believe that the notion that we are called is ridiculous! Keep reading.

Most people believe they have some sort of individual destiny or calling. Maybe you have not given this concept much thought. It could be that you are living your individual destiny and you don't even know it! And while we are talking destiny or calling, know that yours might change, many times, over your lifetime…or it might not change at all.

Over the years, I've met many individuals who were truly living their callings. Work can be a means to an end. But most of us have something that puts a fire in our belly; when we do it, we lose track of time. Imagine what your life would be like if what you called work caused you to be so engrossed in it that you become unaware of time passing.

Book Format

Finally, a bit about the format of this book. Each chapter in this book addresses a different topic. Since we need different things at different times in our lives, I suggest that you read only the chapters that fit for you. You will know what you need and what fits. Save the other chapters for another time or for a friend. If you can, find someone with an open mind who isn't invested in your career to bounce ideas off. Reading and writing and talking about your next move make for a powerful combination.

At the end of each chapter, you will find a section titled *Take Action*. The questions in these sections are designed to make you think about how the material applies to your unique situation. Grab a notebook and plan to do some writing! By answering the questions posed in the *Take Action* section of each chapter, you can start to formulate answers about what your ideal work might be. If you don't like to write, find the right person to talk through the *Take Action* questions with. Better yet, do both! You probably know what your calling is, even if it doesn't seem apparent to you right now.

Take Action

1. Think about the last time you were stuck. This can be in any area of your life and does not need to be work-related. Why were you stuck? What did being stuck do for you? This last one is a big one. Being stuck had a payoff for you.

2. List the work or careers that you have held to date. Include EVERYTHING. Did you deliver papers? Sell beer in the stands at an annual summer event? Don't leave anything off your list. For some, this list will be long. For others, you might only have two or three jobs on your list. This step is important as you will refer to this list as you address future *Take Action* items.

3. List the volunteer experiences that you have had to date. Again, list EVERYTHING. Include walking the neighbor's dog, the committee that you served on that dissolved after just three meetings, and your work as a Scout leader when your neighbor was sick and needed your help for five months.

4. Last, take a few minutes to put check marks next to anything on either list that you truly enjoyed. Don't spend much time thinking about this as you read through your list. Go with your first instinct. When you finish, look at your check marks (if you have any). Do you see patterns or themes? Think about why you checked one listed item and not another. Sit with this for a few minutes and then keep reading.

PART 1

Think It

CHAPTER 1

Do You Have a Calling?

Maybe you believe that you have always had a predestined calling. Or maybe you believe that your life is mostly predetermined. Our society puts a great deal of emphasis on parents and their influence on children. While we know that parents do influence their children, how much of that shaping is external and how much of it is preprogrammed? Whether you believe that your destiny is preprogrammed depends on who you are and your overall value and belief system.

I'm going to share a little story about my own calling and then relate my story to YOU! My own soul's calling felt like destiny. When we have a calling, we keep getting the same message, often through multiple channels. This has been true for me.

In retrospect, my calling may have first surfaced in grade school when I was chosen, without auditioning, from hundreds of students to narrate a school-wide presentation about the city where we lived. I recall being strangely at ease in front of the crowd of parents and classmates although I had spent little time rehearsing for the role. It was obvious that I was comfortable in front of groups of people.

Throughout my childhood, I took piano lessons and often performed at school events and recitals. Although memorizing the pieces was never my forte, the performance felt right to me. I later became a piano teacher while I was still in high school.

I also taught Sunday school, was a counselor at a church camp, and found myself coaching peers at work in my first leadership role at only 19 years of age. As my career progressed, I continued to find myself at the head of the conference room, facilitating discussions and coaching, as we problem-solved. As I moved from one employer to another, I would occasionally take a non-leadership role, only to find myself promoted into some sort of leadership position.

Are you ready for my infamous Burger King story? At one point in my career, I was pondering yet another move and I told someone that I wanted a job taking orders at Burger King. Coincidently, I had worked at McDonalds in high school. But back to Burger King. I had a friend who said, upon hearing my Burger King comment, "You would start out taking orders and in two weeks you'd be managing the damn place!" You see, I like to fix things, lead things, make things better, and act as a cheerleader for others. She was right, although two weeks was an overly aggressive timeline.

In my 20s, I was invited by a local university to teach as an adjunct instructor. It made my heart sing. My interactive classes brought students back to me session after session. My instructor evaluations produced well-above-average markings on a consistent basis. Other universities and vocational schools asked me to teach. It seems like I've been called time and time again to teach. I use the term "teach" loosely since I most enjoy coaching and helping adult students draw on experiences they have had to help them learn and understand new concepts. Now I am a professor and a Career Coach. No surprises there, huh?

Do you see patterns? We are going to look at patterns that you have experienced in your life. When was the last time you listened to what is all around you? Do you pay attention to the hints that pepper your life, your interests, and to what you know intuitively? You likely know what you should be doing in the way of work. Are you doing it?

There are so many ways that you can discover your calling. Here are a few examples.

My husband and I have two friends, both of whom love flying and wanted to become pilots. One, although living on a tight budget with limited disposable income, made an appointment for a flying lesson. He could have read a flight instruction book or done any number of other things to move in the direction of his calling. Even though he didn't really have the money or even the time to pursue his calling, he found a way to make it a reality. For the past 30 years, he has enjoyed his time in the air. He remains a private pilot and he knows that he was meant to fly. Just recently, he started to research careers in aviation. The other friend started talking about becoming a pilot in his teens. He is now in his fifties and continues to TALK about being a pilot. The good news for him is that it is not too late. He can still become a private pilot. It's not too late for you either. The point is, that without moving forward, nothing is going to happen to his dream or to your dream. If you want to move in the direction of your calling, you need to make a move. You need career movement with meaning.

Approaching 30, one woman decided that she wasn't sure where her life was headed. She didn't feel that she had any sort of destiny or calling, and she was frustrated with the direction her life had taken. She found that each day was much like the last. Her energy level was low, and her life seemed to lack purpose. She decided to do something completely out of the ordinary and booked a week at a spa, away from her children and husband. She didn't have the time or the money for an entire week, but felt compelled to find some deeper meaning in her life.

When she left, friends and family thought she was selfish. What would her husband and kids do without her? What did she think she was doing spending money that they didn't have? Where were her priorities? When she returned, she made big changes in her life. She made time to pursue some of her past hobbies, scheduled a medical procedure that she had been contemplating for years, and carved out time to start a new business. Six months after her time away, she paid off the credit card that she used to fund her trip with proceeds from the independent business that she started after returning from her short sabbatical. She used the rest of her proceeds to bulk up a savings account. Her business is based on a passion she had as a child and she finally feels that she is living the life she was meant to live. More than a year has passed and many of the same people who criticized her for deserting her family for a week are now applauding her for finding a way to successfully integrate her calling, passions, home life, and professional life. They say she has never looked better. I don't wonder why!

What is stopping you from finding your destiny or calling?

People who have found their callings all seem to agree that while life isn't necessarily easier, it sure is more rewarding. You have a choice. Make your move now. Experience your Career Yaw.

Take Action

1. Think about what keeps coming up for you in your life. Think about the GOOD stuff. When you sit quietly and listen, do you keep coming back to the same things? Is your life trying to tell you something? Are there patterns? Think about those patterns and what they have looked like in each decade of your life. Whether you are almost 20 or over 70, you will be able to see patterns, if you look for them. Capture your thoughts on paper.

2. Make a list of ten possible callings that you MIGHT have. No editing! Just list the first ten things that come to mind. You might have something vague like "computer games" on your list. Or you might have written something specific like "accountant." Just make a list.

3. Notice other patterns that you have experienced in your lifetime. Have you always earned an "A" in science classes but struggled in English classes? Did you like to ice skate when you were young, later playing hockey in high school? Look for anything that has repeated itself in your lifetime. Write it down.

4. Take a few minutes to review your answers to questions 1, 2, and 3. Look for anything that appears more than once or items that are closely related. Put a check mark by each repetitive item.

CHAPTER 2

Must-Haves

Jill knew what she wanted. She was looking to make a career change in her late 40s. She didn't want to go back to school. She wanted summers off. She wanted to be a government employee for retirement purposes. She wanted evenings free to do her own thing. She took everything she knew she wanted and didn't want, and decided to find a job that met her criteria. She knew that she didn't want to be in sales and she wanted her own space or office at work – she loathed work cubicles. After exploring a variety of options, Jill chose a position as a Health Assistant in the school system. She was willing to work as a substitute if that was what was required for her to get her foot in the door. She did what she needed to do to work her way into the position. The job didn't require a nursing degree, but she knew that she would be paid more if she became an Emergency Medical Technician (EMT). After she had worked in the position long enough to know that it was a good fit, she became an EMT.

I've had an opportunity to work in a variety of industries, including mining. As an office worker (definitely a cushy position as mining jobs go) I was able to work days only… most of the time. For most people in mining, this means hauling our butts out of bed somewhere around 3:30 a.m., maybe earlier, and commuting an hour or more, sometimes on dirt roads. This also means going to bed at a crazy-early time to be able to get up at a crazy-early time. I already know what you are thinking. "Suck it up girl!" Early mornings to me are what processed food is to a personal trainer. When I was teaching full-time on a state university campus, I was happiest when my first class started at 11 a.m. I quickly learned that early mornings kicked my butt, made me grumpy, and caused my family life and my health to suffer in a major way. Now, if a mine wants my services, it is on a consulting basis or at a corporate or town office where my hours don't require me to set four alarms.

Don't underestimate the importance of the environment or any other Must-Haves that appear on your list. Take time to really think about your preferred work schedule, your commute, your work environment – things like whether you want a window in your office or whether you are willing to live the cubical life. Spend time contemplating what you would like your peers to be like, who you would or would not want to work for, and what the absolute non-negotiables are. Is there a certain location that you have in mind? Do you want to work from home? What about pay?

You should consider things as basic as what you want to wear to work as you contemplate what is important to you. I worked with one woman who was certain that she didn't want to work in an environment that required her to adhere to a strict dress code. Uniforms were out of the question. I worked with a man who wanted at least half of his time to be scheduled outside of the office, moving from one job site or location to another. He knew that life behind a desk would put him over the top.

If you have a difficult time thinking about what you really want in a position, you can work the process backward. Think about what you have not liked about past positions and then write the opposite on a piece of paper. Read what you have written and see if it resonates.

It's usually early in the process of career exploration that most of the clients I work with begin to panic for one reason or another. Often, we start to look for patterns or clues about our right line of work and we realize that our current work is WAY off course. If you are one of the lucky ones, your current position gives you at least part of what you are needing in several areas. But often, if someone has decided to work with me, or in your case, if you picked up this book, it is because you have at least a hunch that you are not doing the work that you should be doing. As you continue to dig deeper into options, make lists, and look at what might be right for you, you may find that you are distraught to discover that you are even further away from where you want to be than you first imagined. Don't spend time worrying about it. The fact that you are exploring options is a great first step. Be proud of yourself for working to unearth your right work. This is your Career Yaw. Instead of beating yourself up over time lost, you can view every past position or experience as being one that is bringing you closer to what will feed your soul. How awesome is that?

Get ready for a short note about money. You will read more about money later, but I want you to pause to consider something about the financial piece of work as it relates to your Must-Haves. Sometimes we research career options and make decisions that some line of work won't support the lifestyle that we want, based on demographic data. Data is always helpful, but it is rare that there is not substantial room for growth outside of the salary data that you find when you research a certain career.

Take Action

1. Location, Location, Location. Do you have location constraints? Are they REAL location constraints? This is one of the first Must-Haves that you should consider. If you are not willing to move out of your current home, this is a major consideration. It will limit your options but not as much as you probably think. Start by writing about whether you want to stay where you are. If a move is an option, write about that too.

2. What are at least 15 Must-Haves on your list? Dig deep here, and then go deeper. Once again, don't edit. Instead, write whatever first comes to mind. If your list is longer than 15, keep writing.

You can edit later. If your list only has one or two items on it, think about the aspects of past jobs that you didn't like and write about the opposite to see if opposites make your Must-Have list.

3. Take a few minutes to make a list of Nice-To-Haves. This list will include things that you would really *like* to have. Maybe you want a commute that is 15 minutes or less, but it doesn't make your Must-Have list. Maybe you want to work from your home office. Put it on your Nice-To Have-list. For most of us, the Nice-To-Have list will be longer than the Must-Have list. Include anything that immediately comes to mind.

CHAPTER 3

Looking for Clues

It's time for a little detective work. There are clues all around you.

If you are at a total loss regarding what it is you have been called to do, chances are you haven't been paying attention to all the clues around you that can lead you to be Happy at Work.

I think about my beautiful, talented, near-perfect daughter (just go with me on this). She is incredibly organized, almost unnaturally responsible, and is gifted artistically. There are so many work possibilities for her that would draw on her many talents. She could become an Interior Designer, using her keen eye to help clients create spaces that are unique, beautiful, and efficient. Bonus: She would meet deadlines, stay within the client's budget, and would always deliver as promised. She could go into marketing and use her artful eye to create the next big ad campaign for a Fortune 500 company. If she wants a different lifestyle, she could become an art teacher, helping other people to explore their artistic sides. Of course, another option is for her to explore other work and nurture her artistic side in other ways. I could include another half dozen possible professions as I think about her talents. There are clues all around her!

Do you ever get so excited about something that your words spill out of your brain and you find yourself tangled up in your words and thoughts? Maybe you can hardly wait to tell your friend about the car that you saw at the car show last weekend. You remember every aspect of the car as you spew out details about everything from the logo on the steering wheel to the stitching on the gear shift. These are clues as to what you are passionate about.

Sometimes we don't see the clues around us. Or sometimes we may see them, but they don't resonate with us. And sometimes we see them, they resonate, but we don't know what to do next.

Clues come in many forms. One way that we receive clues is through our physical responses. Mary worked for an employer for about a year before she resigned. She remembers that she felt uneasy about the position during the interview. It wasn't the typical nervousness, but it was an uncomfortable, anxious feeling that she didn't recall having felt in past interviews. When she started working for the organization, she found that she was constantly fighting an upper respiratory infection or an upset stomach. She just didn't FEEL good. And during her year with the employer, her sleep patterns were awful. Some nights she would wake up anxious and find it took her hours to fall back to sleep. Other nights she would just get up at 2 a.m. rather than fight her restlessness. She remembers talking to one of her good friends about the position prior to her start date. She smiled as she reviewed the great benefits package and generous annual salary with the potential for big bonuses. She recalls thinking that something was off. Her emotions just didn't seem to match her smile or her verbal explanation of the position.

Maybe you've had an experience like Mary's?

In the classroom, I like to talk about intuition, which I maintain is largely distilled experience. Think of your brain as a giant, organized filing cabinet. Each time you have an experience, it is filed away. When we call on intuition, we are drawing on the contents of the filing cabinet. We need to pay attention to that gut feeling which is often labeled as intuition. Understanding that all of our distilled experiences are filed away in our brains giving our intuition a place to start reminds us that intuition is more than just a feeling. Tune into your intuition.

**Pay attention to your thoughts, feelings,
and your physical reaction when you are looking for clues.**

Intuition should not be ignored.

Take Action

1. Ask two friends or family members if they see clues around you. Take notes!

2. Pay attention to clues that your body gives you. If something doesn't feel right, pay attention to the feeling. If something feels wonderful, tune in to *that* feeling. Our bodies give us clues all the time. We just need to listen. When was the last time that you did something and felt a lump in your throat or a sick feeling in your stomach? Write about it. What about the last time that you did something, and time got away from you? Write about that too.

CHAPTER 4

Childhood Interests

What were your interests when you were a child? It sounds cliché, doesn't it? But this works. I have a few examples for you.

When I grow up, I want to be a…. What did you want to be when you grew up? What did you say when an adult asked you this giant question and you were two, five, eight, thirteen, or sixteen? Were your answers consistent? Did they change?

When Jack was twelve years old, he spent hours with something called an Erector Set. It was a building kit with bars, bolts, nuts, and connecting pieces, a small motor, and dozens of other parts. The set could be used to build anything from a skyscraper to a helicopter. Jack was only limited by his imagination. He would build a masterpiece and then, sometimes apprehensively, rip it apart so he could build something else. He could spend hours building, never bored, rarely distracted, and never creating the same thing unless it was a much better new and improved version. Jack is an engineer now. He is a happy engineer. In his position, he imagines and then builds things, often on a very small scale prior to something going into production. He builds new and improved versions and, even though not every part of his job appeals to him, more than 70% of his position brings him joy. That is an enviable percentage!

Maybe you liked to bring home wounded animals and nurse them back to health. Did you spend hours playing teacher when you played school?

Or were you the student? When you reached for a book in the school library, what was it likely to be about? When you finished your schoolwork and had free time at school, what would you do?

When asked to draw pictures at school, Barry always included a sailboat in his pictures. Everything he turned in had a sailboat on it. When Barry had water in his picture it was easier to incorporate the sailboat, but he put sailboats in all of his pictures. A picture of a family? A sailboat on a coffee table. A picture of a picnic? A sailboat toy on the blanket. Sometimes Barry had to be very creative. A picture of his dog? A sailboat chew toy. He would even hide little sail boats in some pictures where incorporating one simply wasn't an option. Barry grew up on the coast and his family sailed. I expect that sailing will always be a part of Barry's life.

I've had the pleasure of spending time with an early childhood educator who really, really knows her stuff. She talks about kids' natural talents. These kids are out of diapers, not quite tying their shoes, yet they exhibit natural talents even while they are still learning to zip up their jackets. If you have someone in your life who remembers you as a young child, ask them about the natural talents that you were displaying even before you were able to master anything but pull-up pants.

Take Action

1. Make a list of interests that you had at ages 5, 10, and 15. Do you see themes?

2. Ask a parent, a sibling, or a friend from your K-12 years what they thought you would be when you grew up. Did they see themes and patterns that you have forgotten about?

CHAPTER 5

Whose Dream Is It Anyway?

My father wants me to go into law. My sister thinks I should open a bike shop. My partner wants me to settle into something with traditional office hours and is all about networking on my behalf. Whose dream is it anyway?

When everyone has an agenda for you, it's difficult to focus on your own. If you are not certain about what you want, trust me, someone will decide for you.

We've all watched the movies about the character who follows a dream that belongs to someone else, only to break away from the horrific job and go backpacking with their long-lost love interest. We cheer for the character. They broke away! They followed their heart! Of course, the movie ends, and we don't see what happens a year later.

If you are clear about what you want, other people will still try to tell you what to do. You will nod politely and do what you were going to do anyway before they offered their usually unsolicited advice. If you are not clear about what you want to do, work on clarity. You can ask people who really know you for their opinions. I've pointed out that they might have some ideas that resonate with you and they might even see the right career path for you when you are not able to. Just be conscious of the fact that everyone has their own agenda. When someone has a stake in your life, it is difficult for them to offer advice without considering what might bring the advice-giver a little happiness too.

To get some clarity in this particular area, you will want to consider the goals and aspirations of people who are in your circle of influence. When you ask them for input, or they provide unsolicited advice, ask yourself if what they have said is true for you, or just true for them.

Is it your dream, or their dream?

Trevor was working on his college degree. He knew that he wanted to pursue his dream of becoming a high school shop teacher. His mother had other ideas. The manufacturing plant in the area where Trevor lived had jobs with starting pay that was more than what a teacher would make their first year. Plus, the positions at the manufacturing plant didn't require a college degree. In fact, many of the residents in the town went right from high school into a position at the plant where they had good benefits and pay. There were "lifers" at the plant; people who had been working there for nearly forty years. Trevor's father and older brother worked at the plant. They were happy, and for them, it was their right work. But Trevor was clear that he didn't want to work there. Every time he had a big assignment due or a difficult class that was requiring an unusual amount of his time, his mother would encourage him to get a job at the plant and go to night school. Trevor knew that once he started at the plant, he would probably never finish his degree, and if he did, he would have a difficult time adjusting to a teacher's pay and would be likely to give up his dream. He finally quit telling his mother about the difficult assignments and classes and steered the conversation in another direction when his mother talked about jobs at the factory. He had a dream and it wasn't congruent with his mother's dream. Thank goodness he was strong enough to see what was happening. I'm happy to report that Trevor is a wonderful shop teacher. The students adore him and he provides his students with inspiration and direction. He loves his work and can see himself in his current role far into the future. I should note that Trevor's brother is equally happy with his job at the manufacturing plant. He likes the stability and the schedule which makes it possible for him to fly fish almost every day. One career is not better than the other, but one career can be good for one person and bad for another.

Sometimes the fears that the adults in our lives are carrying spill over into our lives. Sometimes they are apparent. Meron's father often talked about all the things that Meron could not do. He would talk about lack, limitation, and roadblocks. There were a multitude of external factors that would make it so Meron could never do what he wanted to do, at least according to his father. Then there was the internal stuff. His father would talk about how Meron just didn't have the brainpower to do something. He would explain that Meron had always been clumsy and surely would not succeed in his latest bid to go out for a new sport. Meron's father was using his own script to try to create Meron's script. Meron was creative and smart and had the intelligence to do whatever he wanted to do. Maybe his father didn't have those same skills and was projecting his stuff on to Meron? And that one time that Meron tripped that his father would not let him forget about? Yup. Meron's father was a jerk. We all trip from time to time.

True is 35 and he has already changed careers six times since graduating from high school and then college. He wants to shift careers again, but his family and friends all give him crap about bouncing around from one profession to another. Most of us have responsibilities and we need to take into consideration what others depend on us for, especially our children. If True can bounce and is happy while maintaining a good salary and the benefits that his family needs, maybe his family should be bouncing with him?

To determine if the dream belongs to you or to someone else, find someone without a vested interest in your work. Someone on the outside who won't be directly affected by the decisions you make is much more likely to help you follow your right path. It's your decision. It's your life. You can be Happy at Work.

Take Action

1. Consider your board of directors; the people in your life who would sit at your table. This might include influential teachers, friends, relatives, or leaders. Draw an oval on the page and make seats at your table. Label the seats with your board of director's names.

2. Next, consider why each of the people listed on your board of directors made your list.

3. Next to each board member, list anything that they may have wanted or still want you to be.

4. Are you living your dream or their dream?

CHAPTER 6

Near-Death

Some of us had to have a near-death experience to make the right career changes. You don't have to do that to experience a Career Yaw. You can do it now.

In 2014, I was diagnosed with Triple Negative Breast Cancer. I'll spare you the details. It's enough for you to know that my treatment was turbo-aggressive. While I was going through my treatment, one of my friends, Gina, also was diagnosed. Although she had another kind of breast cancer, we moved through mastectomies, chemotherapy, reconstruction, and all of the shit that peppered our experiences, together. Yet another friend, Tiffany, had just been through diagnosis and the same process. She acted as our guide and cheerleader.

I'm happy to report that as I sit here writing, Tiffany, Gina, and I are all cancer-free. We are still learning, but here are some of the takeaways from our experiences that might be helpful to you on your personal career journey.

Celebrate All Things: Smile. Rejoice. Life is beautiful. Make everyday life a special occasion.

Maintain Healthy Relationships: Some relationships are not worth hanging on to. All relationships have something to teach us. We are all messy. Forgive, but don't necessarily hang on. Refuel with positive friends and people. Limit time-sucking relationships. Build people up.

Do What Makes You High: Where is your happy place? What do you love to do?

We All Have a Story: Part of our story is cancer, although for each of us, it isn't our front page. What is your story? Will you leave your own legacy? Let go of the albatross that hangs around your neck. Write your story. You have choices.

Work: Love what you do! Love the people you do it for and work with. If you aren't in love with your work, make damn sure that it meets all of your other needs and find something that you love that your work supports – perhaps a hobby or a cause.

Abundance: It's all around us. This is not necessarily related to possessions. Give back. This includes your time and talents. Cultivate joy. Consider how much is enough.

God or Your Higher Power: There is always hope. Find your home. God knows your name.

Do It Now: I know someone who says that if her cancer returns, she is going to drink champagne in her greenhouse every day. I think I need to head over to her greenhouse to drink champagne with her at least once each week to celebrate life! Is your desire a trip, a degree, visiting a relative, or making peace? Do it NOW. Dream – but *Take Action* too!

Trust Yourself: You already have the answers to whatever you are questioning. Trust your gut. Intuition, after all, includes distilled experiences. It is your gut on steroids.

How does this simple list translate to career choices? Some of it is obvious. Some of it is less obvious. But here is a rough translation for you.

Celebrate the ordinary. Look for the extraordinary. Do what you love and love what you do (thanks Life is Good®). Do not wait. Do it now. Today. I repeat, DO NOT WAIT.

Take Action

1. What do you celebrate? Are you celebrating what is most important to you?

2. Think for a moment about what you want to be able to say about your career when you look back on your life. Write a paragraph summarizing what you want to be able to say. It might be very specific. It might be general. Just write it. And then read it. Read it again.

3. What do you talk about doing but never quite get around to doing? Why aren't you doing it? How could you make doing it a reality in the next year?

CHAPTER 7

The Stories We Tell Ourselves

I had a captive audience. I was standing in a classroom with about 50 students. They were ready for a lecture. The subject was Recruitment and Staffing. The lectures were mostly geared toward the employer and organizational end of things. These students were here to learn about Recruitment and Staffing so they could be better leaders in their organizations. The topic for this lecture was Interviews. I knew that the students, who were adults ages 18 to 67, were going to have some great stories to share…stories from their employment experiences and, although they didn't know it yet, stories they were telling themselves.

We started with the material from the text. We covered all of the relevant topics related to interview preparation. Next, students shared their interview horror stories. They talked about experiences from the perspective of the interviewer as well as experiences from the perspective of the interviewee. Most had examples of what should not happen during an interview. I reminded them that social media has increased sharing of such experiences and we discussed why employers need to be very concerned about the interview process and how it might influence the company brand.

When I asked the students if they thought that workers in the United States were more or less satisfied with their work than they were five years ago, the majority of students said that workers were less satisfied with their work.

It was time to flip things around. I asked four questions.

1.   Have you changed jobs in the past two years?

2.   If so, is your new job an improvement over your past job?

3.   Do you know what you would REALLY like to do for work?

4.   Are you doing what you would REALLY like to do?

More than half of the students in the classroom had changed jobs in the past two years. Nearly all of those students thought that their new job was an improvement over their past job. This meant that they were more satisfied with their work than they were five years ago. Keep in mind that these same students reported that workers, in general, were less satisfied with their work now than they were two years ago.

We took a deeper dive and moved on to the next question. When asked, "Do you know what you would REALLY like to do for work?", a surprising 80% of the students said that they knew what they would REALLY like to do. Given that high response, I was shocked that only 10% of the students were doing what they really wanted to do, especially after more than half of the students had just reported that they were more satisfied at work now as compared to five years ago.

This is where things took a turn. I asked those who were comfortable sharing, why they were not doing what they REALLY wanted to do. The answers fell into several categories, two of which were most common. Students either thought that they did not have the right education or they believed that they could not make enough money doing the job they REALLY wanted.

The first response was no surprise. The students, after all, were in the class to earn a degree. Many had been told that they would not be able to move up in their organization without a degree. They needed the degree to be promoted or they needed the degree to switch to another field of work. We spent some time talking about this because, although this was likely a real barrier to entry for many of them, there can be workarounds that vary by industry.

It was the second response that best illustrates Stories We Tell Ourselves. There are many reasons why money might be a barrier but it does not have to be. I divided the students into small groups, and they discussed ways that they might be able to change the story without going on a meal plan that involved copious amounts of peanut butter and jelly sandwiches and an address change that involved the attic of their Great Aunt's house.

Their ideas were wonderfully creative. A student who had always worked both a full-time and a part-time job talked about how the full-time job always was the moneymaking position while the part-time work was the job they REALLY wanted. In time, he hoped to make the part-time job his full-time work.

I have many friends who are full-time professors and teachers. Most of them teach because they love the work. Most of them also do something on the side to "support their teaching habit." I have one friend who is a waiter at a restaurant during the busy summer travel season. She loves visiting with the customers and she rakes in the tips! I have another friend who picks up at least one substantial consulting gig each summer, using her expertise in her area of study to bring in some extra dough. Another friend who is allergic to grass (the kind in front of houses) has a lawn business. Yes, a lawn business! She is an entrepreneur, saw a need in her community, and decided that it was time to fill that need. She doesn't cut any lawns, but she has a crew of five that are busy all summer long and she makes a tidy sum with her summer business.

Here are some examples of ways that you might make some money outside of your chosen career to support your work habit. If you are mechanically inclined, you could offer mechanical services after your regular work hours or on your days off. If you have an interest in music, you might work as a DJ on the side. If you like to bake, see what you need to do to sell your famous almond bark at the local gift shop. If you have a special ability to craft, find out what you would need to do to hold a holiday crafting day where participants pay to attend and walk away with a gift-worthy finished project.

Many professions are tied to billable hours. There are only so many billable hours in a week. Consider clumping hours together for multiple clients. Terry started offering four-hour seminars in his field to groups of 15 to 20 clients. For those four hours, Terry was making his rate multiplied by the number of participants less his expenses. Instead of charging $140 per hour, Terry was making over $2,100 an hour, less expenses.

Simone is a teacher and provides group tutoring sessions two days each week after school. He charges $25 per student and schedules five to seven students for each two-hour block of time. At five students, he is making $125 an hour. The subject is the same for all of the students and, while he provides each student with some one-on-one instruction, he finds that the students are sharing best practices and helping each other too.

Boyd is a great mechanic. He offers hands-on sessions once each month at the local community college, teaching car owners how to make simple repairs. He didn't think it would catch on in his community, but his great sense of humor combined with his natural teaching abilities has made it necessary for him to cap his sessions at a maximum of ten participants. He negotiated with the community college and receives half of the collected fees in a lump sum payment for his sessions. Many of the participants visit Boyd at his shop for things they cannot fix themselves because of the relationship he forged with them during his how-to sessions. They trust him.

What about making more in your primary position while doing what you love? It is SO realistic to do this. Think about it. You probably know personal trainers who eke out a living and constantly complain that clients are not willing to pay them what they deserve for their services. You can probably list three celebrity trainers, even if you aren't into the whole personal trainer scene, who are making big bucks. Know that there are thousands of trainers who fall somewhere between these two extremes. We see this in every profession. You probably are aware of a CPA who makes only a modest living and can likely think of others who are very comfortable and have dozens of other CPAs working for them. I know people in food service who make $35,000 annually and others who make more than $100,000 annually. This can be said of nearly every profession. If you are not on the high end of your earning potential, what can you do to change things?

Take Action

1. Make a list of the stories you tell yourself. Write "I can't" at the top of your paper and then list anything that comes to mind. Now go back to your list and turn it around. Include three ways that you could or can for each of the can't items. Don't edit. Just write.

2. When you think about your work, write three things that you consider to be personal weaknesses. You might be able to think of more than three, but start with just three. Now brainstorm ways that you might compensate for them. If you have no problem making money but are not good at managing it, could you hire someone to help you manage your money? If you tend to give services away at discounted rates, could you have

someone else handle your billing? If you are lacking negotiating skills and you need them in your position, can you take a class, read a book, or meet with a friend who is a great negotiator to explore ways that you might improve your skillset?

CHAPTER 8

Full Circle

When you don't pay attention to what you already know, you end up spinning your wheels and usually end up right where you started.

Joan knew when she was in high school that she wanted to be a police officer. Her father was in law enforcement, and she had the right personality to make it in the business. She knew what she wanted to do.

Enter, life. In college, Joan ended up taking some classes to explore some other options. None of them really stuck to the wall for her, but she eventually started to work on a degree in an entirely different field. Joan wasn't even really certain about how this all happened. Nearly 120 credit hours later, she admitted that what she really wanted was a degree in Criminal Justice and a career in law enforcement.

There is nothing wrong with looking into other interests. In fact, it is possible that what you thought you wanted isn't what you should really be doing. Maybe you were not even aware of other options that were available to you, but instead selected a career path based on what you thought you could do, based on what others wanted you to do, or based on a passing interest. Sometimes you are derailed for a reason, and in the end, your alternate path ends up being the right path. But sometimes it doesn't.

Joan knew all along that she really wanted to be in law enforcement. She was certain of it. Even after she started moving in another direction, she found herself drawn to stories about policing. She supported community law enforcement and volunteered in the field. She finally came full circle and pursued what was true for her all along. She is now working in, you guessed it, law enforcement.

What do you already know? You are probably thinking, if you already KNEW, you wouldn't be reading this book! But it is entirely possible that you DO know, and you are not paying attention.

Are you listening to what you already know? Pay attention to what you already know to experience your Career Yaw.

Take Action

1. Make a list of ten things you know for sure. These don't have to be career related. Just start writing. Maybe you know that you like to write. Maybe you know that you enjoy your dog.

2. Next, make a list of ten things you know for sure about who you are as a person. The list may include traits or factual things about the life you are living. Maybe you are a quick learner. Maybe you love to run.

3. Now make a list of ten things that you know about past jobs you've had or your current position. Don't edit. Just write. Maybe you hated working weekends. Maybe you need a workspace with natural light. Maybe you don't like to supervise others.

4. Last, make a list of ten things that you know about your future career. This might include whether you want to work indoors or outdoors. Maybe you want to do something that doesn't involve working on a big team. If you need to, look back at

PART 2

Do It

CHAPTER 9

Getting Unstuck

Are you stuck? If you are, what is in it for you? Ouch! Did that hurt? I bet it did. I will ask you again, if you are stuck, what is in it for you?

There is something is in it for you.

You wouldn't be stuck if there wasn't some sort of payoff or kickback that you were getting.

Thomas complains about his job pretty much every day. He has been in dentistry for a LONG time and is very successful. He diversifies, looks for appropriate niches in his field, and prospers while many of his peers feel lucky to be making half of what Thomas makes every year. Thomas has been in dentistry since he finished his program of study. He isn't happy. Thomas grumbles about every single aspect of his work. Nothing is ever quite right or good enough. He talks about doing something else, even starts other projects that might propel him into another profession, but he never follows through. He is mired in cured cement.

I've asked Thomas what is in it for him? He gives me a half-baked answer. The money is good, the hours are okay, he "knows" it, it feels safe. He doesn't really have to do much to keep the ship heading in the right direction. Apparently, it's good enough. Or is it?

If it were good enough, wouldn't he quit griping about his job? These are difficult questions. Sometimes, when we take stock of what is in it for us, the answer might be to suck it up and quit bitching. The payoff might be so great that we aren't willing to change. If you make the decision that you are not willing to do what it will take to get unstuck, then stop complaining and focus on something else. If you decide that you really do want to get unstuck, put your complaining on hold and work through the *Take Action* sections of this book.

When I was working on my dissertation, a necessary evil for me to earn my doctoral degree, I got stuck BIG TIME. I thought I was going to be imbedded in cement forever, covered in bird poop – another ABD (all but dissertation) casualty. What did I do? I brought out the big guns. I hired a coach, met with her weekly, and set goals. She held me accountable, and I did crazy things to finish the damn dissertation. I checked into a hotel just minutes from my house one weekend with my computer, a printer, those giant flip chart post-it-note things, markers, snacks, and other writing supplies. I unplugged the television in the room and swore off the internet except for research purposes, and I shook the birds off. Then I started to drill holes in the cement. At one point the room looked like a storm had passed through with flip chart post-it notes on the walls and recipe cards stuck to the giant post-it notes, papers strewn across the floor, and open boxes of crackers lining the perimeter. But guess what? I moved forward. And each week after that, I progressed some more. And I finished the damn dissertation, which was necessary for the work that I wanted to do next. I did this while working full-time, teaching on the side, volunteering in my community, and raising a young daughter. It was completely insane, but I did it.

What do you need to break through the imaginary concrete wall? Do you need a coach and hotel room for the weekend and some giant-ass post-it notes? Only you can figure it out. If you are stuck, you need to do whatever is necessary to become free, or else release your need to complain. I hope you opt for the post-it notes instead.

Change can be scary. If you need help deciding what it is that you need to do to become unstuck, consider either or both of the following.

Hire a coach. Sometimes you just need a fresh, professional set of eyes and ears. A good therapist might be able to help you too. They work to help people become unstuck in other areas – a career isn't much different than many of the other areas that they might otherwise address.

Change ONE thing. It doesn't need to be related to your career for it to work. If the whole career direction thing seems too big or too confusing to you right now, commit to a change in another area of your life and table your job situation for a few weeks or a few months. Put a reminder on your calendar to come back to this in 30, 60, or 90 days. You don't get to put this off for more than 90 days. In the meantime, address something on your list right now that might just get you moving in a direction that could trickle into other areas of your life.

George wanted to move into a career that involved publishing a book but just could not seem to get moving in that direction. He decided to take a break from writing and really focus intensely on another goal. He wanted to lose 30 pounds. He started exercising regularly and made healthy eating his top priority. He attacked his weight loss goal and, as he started to lose weight, first six pounds, then 11, then 15, he found himself feeling like he could do other things that seemed unattainable too. I'm pleased to report that George is 35 pounds lighter AND has his manuscript in its final stages. He needed to start somewhere else to get to where he wanted to be, and as a bonus, he is healthier, happier, and moving in several positive directions in multiple areas of his life.

Take Action

1. Ask yourself the following questions. Write at least one paragraph answering each one.

   a. What is being stuck doing for you?

   b. What are you afraid of?

   c. What is the worst possible outcome related to your fears?

   d. What is the best possible outcome related to your fears?

2. Decide to change ONE thing today that is not related to the area where you are stuck. Commit to this one change. Map it out on your calendar. Make it happen.

CHAPTER 10

Noise in the Communication Model: Knowing but not Listening

Maybe you took a speech class in junior high or high school. Maybe you took a communications class in college. Or maybe you didn't. Regardless, you have probably been exposed to the communication model that looks something like this:

Sender - Encoded Message - Message Channel - Decoded Message – Receiver - Feedback

Think about that childhood game where you sat in a circle with other kids and the first child received a message, perhaps from a teacher. The kid whispered the message into the next kid's ear who whispered it into the next kid's ear and the message traveled around the circle until the last one shared the original message with the group. Except that it wasn't the original message! Maybe the message started out as, "The elephant liked to eat peanuts" and ended up, "The little ant hiked to reach farts". Okay, the farts are a stretch, but children like to insert words that make them giggle and seem a little bit naughty.

The part in the communication model that isn't included above is noise. If you look at communication models online, you will also find noise, usually hovering above the model. Noise influences the entire process. Noise can be audible like a bell, or someone talking, or music in the background. A noise could be something else like a flickering light, a thought in our heads, or a physical need such as hunger. Noise makes it difficult for us to hear the message, either because of the audible noise or because we are preoccupied by something else.

We experience noise in every area of our lives. Unfortunately, the noise gets louder when we are contemplating something big. When thinking about a career change, what we want to do with our lives, or what comes next, the chatter can get really loud. It takes on many forms. We hear the opinions of our parents, siblings, colleagues, peers, friends, extended family, and teachers. We also have voices in our heads! Those voices might include things we've been taught, past conversations that we've had, and the stories that we tell ourselves.

Noise can be useful. Noise helps us to learn from past mistakes. It can cheer us on and propel us forward. It can help us weigh advantages and consider disadvantages. Noise can also be counterproductive. It can even cause us to walk away from something that could be wonderfully life changing.

Take Action

1. When the message makes its way around the circle, it tends to change. Think about the messages you tell yourself. Have you altered those messages over time? Is what you tell yourself now true, or did you make it fit?

2. What noise influences your career decisions? Write about the audible noise, the things that you can hear. Then write about the inaudible noise. What are your flickering lights?

3. What are you willing to do about your message? About your noise?

CHAPTER 11

Start Small... Or Big!

A few years ago on my way to work, I saw a trailer with a sign on it that advertised coffee. I drove on by without stopping. A few days later, driving by the same trailer, I saw a few cars parked nearby and a couple of customers at the window. Again, I didn't stop. After a few weeks of noticing the trailer nearly every morning on my way to work, I decided to pull up and see what all the fuss was about. A young woman in her late 20s was selling coffee. She had several offerings, all of the right licenses, and had found a business owner who would let her park on his property. In less than a year, she had opened a café in the strip mall next to the piece of land where she had been selling coffee out of a trailer. She decided that the area needed a coffee shop. She found a way to do it. She took a leap into the unknown and it paid off. Her shop is buzzing with caffeinated clientele on a daily basis. She knows her java!

She started small. She ended up big. I'm waiting for her to open her second shop.

It doesn't matter whether you start small or start big. Just start.

There are many ways to begin. One way is by creating space.

Create mental space. If your head is too full of to-do lists, schedules, and data, then you need to create some mental space. If you haven't tried meditation, do it now! It really works. By taking even five minutes each day to clear your mind, you create space for other things to manifest themselves.

If you aren't the meditating type, or just the thought of meditation makes you cringe, consider your own brand of meditation. Do you knit? Do you paint? Do you get into your zone when you clean? You are already meditating in your own way.

Finally, you need to create space in the way of time. This serves several purposes. By creating space to work through the *Take Action* items in this book, you are making space for your new career.

Another place to start might be with your physical space. Maybe creating order is your first action item before you do anything else. Perhaps you decide to clean out a walk-in closet and put only a chair in it. Or maybe you need a space with a small desk? Find a corner where you can set up a place that is truly yours.

Most of our lives are wonderfully full. If your life is so busy that you have little in the way of space, you might not have enough room, literally, for new ideas, direction, and career options to take hold. You might need to loosen up some space to let your next career work its way in.

Historically, I am terrible at creating space, at least in some areas. I'm pretty good at reorganizing my physical space, but I seem to need to work at it all the time. Your physical space may be too full to let anything else in. If it is full of stuff – papers, furniture, clutter, or chaos, you won't have room to breathe, much less room to let anything new in. Create physical space and notice what happens. When you have physical space that is open, other things come into your life; not physical things, but other good things.

There are two ways to get into the waters of change. If you want to, you can jump in and adjust to the water when you hit it. Years ago, I went to school with Mike. Mike jumped off the work cliff. He was a CEO for a company, and over a period of a few months, became increasingly disgruntled with the parent company's attempts to become more involved in operations. We talked about his challenges. He knew it was time for him to make a change and wanted to shift careers entirely. My advice? Flesh out the details of your career change while you are working. No need to jump off the cliff. Mike didn't listen. One afternoon he called me and told me that he had just resigned, packed up his office, and walked out. It was what he needed to do.

Maybe you are not a cliff jumper. Neither was one of my past coworkers, Noah. He was in a conservative profession, had a great position, and liked his work. Because he was intuitive and knew his business, he could see that the life cycle of the product he was working with would stall out in about two years. He loved to brew coffee...really fabulous, toe-curling, over-the-top coffee. He used a special blend of beans and a unique roasting process. I know little about coffee, but even I could tell that his was something special when I tasted it. Noah is making plans to produce and sell his magic brew. He is working with another successful entrepreneur who has launched two wildly profitable ventures in the past decade so that he can fine-tune his plans. I believe that Noah will make it big as I watch him carefully plan each aspect of his coffee business. Noah started by dipping his toe into the water. Next, he carefully lowered one leg, just up to mid-shin. No cliff jumping for Noah.

Take Action

1. Are you a cliff jumper or a toe dipper? Given both options, which would you prefer? Why?

2. Once you determine your preferred style, think about actions you could take today, this week, and this month, to prepare to jump or to just dip your toe in the water.

3. Brainstorm five possible actions that fit into each of the three categories as you consider your Career Yaw; today, this week, and this month.

CHAPTER 12

Young Adults

It's crazy that we expect young adults in their mid to late teens to make decisions that will influence what they do for a lifetime. The reality is that most teens don't have a clue about what they want to do. If they do, it's more likely to be what their parents' or a mentor's vision is for them. If this sounds like you, you may be thinking that you might as well just give up. If you are a parent and are ready to find me online and give me a piece of your mind, know that even though our expectations as a society for young adults are unrealistic, there are ways to increase the probability that someone in this age group can find the right career path or area to study, despite the societal pressures.

This past year I was fortunate enough to get to work with Ben. Ben was a high school senior who decided that he was going to go into the military, a great career and life move that serves many young adults well. The thing is, he didn't really WANT to go into the military. He was an average student at best, with a father and three older brothers who didn't graduate from high school, and a younger brother who showed academic promise. Ben assumed that there really weren't any other career options for him, outside of a job at a local grocery store. Ben told me that he had never even considered college, and that any money his family had, really needed to be used for his younger brother's education because he was smarter than Ben.

I started working with Ben, first by simply making him aware that college really was an option if it held any interest for him. I started with a few comments about possibilities. An amazing thing happened. In spite of a learning disability, Ben's grades started to climb. He started to complete his schoolwork and turn it in on time. He started to dream about what he would do if he could really do anything he wanted to do. We started to look at all of the possibilities. We looked at his athletic abilities and explored scholarship options. We looked at schools, mostly public, and the programs that they offered. We talked openly about his disability and what might be available to him in the way of assistance. We started to explore OPTIONS. Most importantly, he started to see OPTIONS.

As I write this, Ben is a college student in a two-year program. He plans to transfer into a four-year institution to study a business-related career. We were able to find funding assistance and scholarships for all but a small portion of his tuition and books. Not only is he the first male in his immediate family to earn a high school diploma, but he is the first male in his family to attend college. Ben would tell you that it isn't a fairytale life he is living. He has to work hard for his grades and he studies more than he ever has. He must plan his week around his school and work commitments (yes, he also works more than 30 hours each week). He lived at home his first year of college when he would have preferred to be out on his own. But he has a plan and is doing something he never imagined possible. He needed someone to help him through the process (see the chapter titled, *Get Some Help Already!*).

Ben is also working the multiple career options angle. In the midst of all of this, Ben doesn't realize that I am also going to encourage him to do some coaching in his sport. This could give him a third possible career avenue. He won't ever be stuck doing a job that sucks the life out of him, unless he chooses to do so. The decision will be his – not someone else's.

If you have a high school junior or senior in your life who seems to be struggling with what is next, consider paying for a few career coaching sessions for him or her. It's a gift that could truly change your student's life!

There are many resources available to high school and college students that few take advantage of. Here are just a few of them.

- Visit your school's Career Center.

- Take tests to narrow your interests. These might be called interest inventories or they might be personality tests. Ask your Career Center who administers these tests at your school.

- Check out the Boys and Girls Club or a similar organization in your area. They may have resources available to help you as you consider what would make you Happy at Work.

- Take advantage of free tours at various public and private universities. Ask if the university allows potential students access to any of the Career Services offered at the university.

- Ask one or two of your favorite teachers if they would meet with you after school to talk about career options.

- Ask family members and friends if you can visit with them to discuss their careers. Inquire why they went into their chosen field and what they like and don't like about it.

- Do some research! Read about careers that interest you. Is additional education after high school required for entry level positions in fields that interest you. Learn what the average rates of pay are for the position. Look for people who do the work that interests you and ask them if you can schedule an informational interview to learn more about their career path. An informational interview

Take Action

1. If you are a young adult, make an appointment today (it might take you a few weeks to get in to see someone) to do ONE of these things: visit your school's career center, take an interest inventory or personality test, tour a university, meet with a teacher, or visit with a family member or friend about their career.

2. If you are a parent, guardian, or friend of a young adult who is considering career options, schedule a time to talk about their interests and what they might do to explore their opportunities.

3. Visit https://www.bls.gov/ooh/ and spend some time researching career options. This free resource is updated frequently.

CHAPTER 13

Back to School

Should you go back to school? It depends. For some careers you need a very specific degree. For other careers, additional education is nice to have. Although I am admittedly a huge advocate for higher education, I also recognize that some of the most successful people I know either do not have a college degree, or have a college degree which has nothing to do with what they ended up doing.

It's time for you to do additional research. Does your area of interest require a degree? If so, what type of degree? Are there jobs within your area of interest that do not require a degree? Will a certification be sufficient? If so, can you complete the certification through self-study and testing? Would someone entering your chosen profession start out in a much better position, or move up much more quickly in the organization with a degree?

If you decide to start or return to school, begin by considering every possible option. Look at your local community colleges and state universities. Consider a private college. Look at the multitude of quality programs of study that are available online. Is there an accelerated program that interests you? Do you need an associate, a bachelor's, a master's, or a doctoral degree? If you have a university degree, do you need a certification too?

Lucinda knew what she wanted to do. She had a degree, but the degree didn't really apply to the position that she was interested in. She researched several options and finally decided to earn a certification which, combined with her undergraduate degree, would give her credibility in her new profession. She was able to find several reputable accredited programs and selected one that someone in her future field of work had recommended to her. She worked out a schedule to complete the program and put everything on her calendar. Then she contacted a friend who she knew would hold her accountable and promised to check in weekly to update her friend on her progress. If Lucinda did not check in, her friend had permission to contact her and ask two questions that Lucinda crafted prior to starting the program. The questions were designed to remind Lucinda about her end goal and to motivate her to get back on track.

There are so many educational options that were simply not available, even a decade ago. Some are formal and some are informal. Many are online. Geographic constraints played a big part in decisions around education in the past, but many of those limitations no longer exist.

Most employers recognize that while a degree or certification shows some mastery of specific skills, it also provides the student with opportunities to improve other marketable skills including communication, teamwork, and critical and analytical thinking. It also shows that a job candidate is self-disciplined and has time management skills.

Take Action

1. Would you consider pursuing additional education for a career? If the answer is no, write a short paragraph about why you are not interested. This is valuable information! If the answer is yes, what are you willing to consider? Would you be willing to attend a one-day seminar, a 10-week course, an entire program of study, or a two-day workshop? List any options that come to mind.

2. If your answer was yes, are you geographically bound to a specific location? If so, research program options in that location. If you are not geographically bound, would you be willing to relocate for the right opportunity? Write a paragraph about your geographic preferences.

CHAPTER 14

Making a Change As a Card-Carrying Adult

Lisa is a rock star in my eyes. In her early 50s, she decided that she had always wanted to be a pilot for a commercial airline. She sat down and figured out what she needed to do. She had spent a good chunk of her life in academia and also had a private pilot's license. That was it. Determined to follow her dream, at a station in life when most of us would freak out over such a big change, she started to work on her other ratings and licenses that she would need to meet her goal. After spending about a year, working on her licenses while continuing to work at her academic job, she started applying for positions. Lisa found a commercial airline that was willing to put her through a crazy-rigorous, three-month-long training program. A large percentage of the other students in the program didn't make it through. They dropped like flies. Lisa studied like a madwoman, eating, drinking, and sleeping in a tangled web of books and training materials. During those three months, she did almost nothing else. Lisa is a pilot now – a wonderfully competent pilot for a commercial airline. She is Happy at Work.

Would you have the courage to give up something you knew, including a secure position, to follow a dream?

I can only imagine the kind of courage it took for Lisa to leave her stable job and pursue her dream. It is both bone-chilling and invigorating. It had to be a huge leap of faith for her, especially as she saw her peers being dropped from the program as they were unable to complete the training.

Nora loved to help people. Nora had an undergraduate degree in business and worked in an office setting but found herself volunteering at a mental health center after hours and occasionally on weekends. It was there that she decided to explore a possible career as a marriage and family counselor. It took her several years, but she completed the coursework and the hours of supervised counseling experience required. She is now a licensed family therapist.

By now you have figured out that I have had multiple careers in many different fields and have tried on many different professions. Sometimes I did things that were placeholders. They allowed me to make money so I could go to school to pursue my passion or let me try on certain aspects of a job to see how it fit. Sometimes I was limited, at least in part, because of where I lived although that usually isn't a valid excuse now. With the internet and the global economy if you have high speed internet and access to a computer, many of the only true limits you have are those that you put on yourself.

When I teach a class, I always start out with an introduction. Part of what I tell students or an audience is why I am qualified to teach a class or speak on a subject. Years ago, I had more than a few professors who had studied a field but they had never worked in it. I hated those classes. The professors would regurgitate crap from textbooks. It was obvious to me and my fellow students that they really hadn't lived the subject; they just knew about it. They quickly lost credibility with their audience.

Fast forward to the present. I want my students or audience to know that I have lived whatever it is I am talking to them about. It's not just theory. I freaking DID IT. I am a professor. I am a master career shifter. I wrote a dissertation about executives who reposition their careers. I continue to publish articles about career shifts and transitions. I have helped many students and working adults figure out what they wanted to do in their professional lives. I have decades of experience working as a human resource professional; screening applicants for positions, offering people jobs, and studying what does or doesn't make someone happy at work. I have lived, breathed, and watched this work stuff for a very long time and have studied it from pretty much every angle.

Change is scary, but once you find your passion, everything starts to shift.

Demetria, a lawyer, never really enjoyed her work. She was good at what she did, but every Sunday she would start to experience the dread that she associated with returning to the practice on Monday. Once her kids entered high school, she decided to make a change. She is now a contractor. She has never been happier. Finding her calling wasn't hard. Claiming it was the hard part. She experienced her Career Yaw in her early 40s and has been happier, less stressed, and more fulfilled. After a few years, Demetria was able to exceed the annual income that she had been making as an attorney. A bonus? Her legal experience with contracts and a multitude of other duties associated with her construction company puts her ahead of her competitors.

Take Action

1. Dream big. If you could have any career you wanted, what would it be? List at least five things that you would do now if you already had the necessary background, including the education and training needed, to be successful.

2. Look at the list and create a second one that includes three career possibilities that fit into each of the categories that you just wrote down. If your initial list included rock star, your second list might include songwriter, musician, music teacher, vocal coach, and performer.

3. Think about how you might transition from what you are doing now to what you would like to be doing. Create a rough timeline and consider the costs associated with the transition. While we dream, we also need to be somewhat realistic.

CHAPTER 15

Reinvention

You might say, "But I have this biology degree and it is all I know!" Is it? It isn't unusual for us to look at the formal training we've had or the jobs that we have held in the past and think that what we are doing or have done doesn't really apply to anything else. You can have four or five completely different "perfect" careers in a lifetime. Many times, one could not have happened without the other.

Meriam was in accounting but always had an interest in the human resource field. We talked about how she could make the transition from one field to another. Meriam had experience with payroll in her accounting position as well as a degree in accounting. In every organization, payroll is either directly or indirectly linked to human resources. Meriam started by looking for a job in payroll that would allow her to grow into a human resource position. Both her payroll experience and accounting coursework enabled her to study and test for a human resource certification. After a year in her payroll position, and with her certification, she moved into an entry level leadership position in her organization's human resource department. Go Meriam!

Sometimes an intermediate job makes the most sense. Greg wanted to work as a management analyst. He didn't have experience in the field and knew it could be a tough field to get into. He had taken some relevant classes at a university and had researched positions in the industry, but he didn't have the right degree or background. Still, he knew he would be good in the position based on past recommendations that he had made to his employers to improve efficiency. He had statistics to back him up! He needed to get his foot in the door. Greg decided to apply for a position as an administrative assistant, reporting directly to a respected management analyst. It wasn't his dream job, but he knew that if he could work with a professional, he could learn more about the field and take on additional responsibilities over time. After an aggressive job search and several interviews, he was offered a position. It didn't pay what he needed, so he worked a part-time job on the side. It took nearly three years, but he moved into a full-time management analyst position and was able to quit his part-time job. He loves his work and would tell you that taking the intermediate position was the best move he could have made.

Ava did things a little bit differently. She had been in a high-stress position for too long. She was good at what she did, but she was exhausted. When her company was sold, she decided it was time to leave and recalibrate. Ava took a job in a completely different field that was, as many of her friends explained to her, "beneath her." Having worked in a demanding leadership position for many years, she took a support position with no supervisory responsibilities. The job was perfect! She no longer had any stress in her position. She was celebrated for her incredible ability to organize things and make things happen. Everyone at her new place of employment adored her. She used the time in the position to focus on other areas of her life, including her health and her family. She spent two years in the support position before she decided that she was ready to move back into her former field of work. The time away allowed her to realize what she was willing, and not willing, to do when she re-entered her profession. Ava returned energized and ready for what was next. She experienced career movement with meaning.

Geography can come into play here too! Maybe you are moving with a partner or have decided on a geographic area, but you aren't quite sure what you will do in your new community. You know where you are going to live but have no idea what this will mean for your career.

Assess this opportunity and see it for what it is! Go back to your list of must-haves and start there.

Leon moved with a family member to a new state without clear direction regarding his career. He liked what he had been doing, but it didn't excite him anymore. He felt like he had learned everything he could learn in his past position and wanted something that was challenging. He did something simple. He created a list of things that might interest him. It included options that would allow him to build on the skills that he already had and what he referred to as "wild options"; options that didn't seem to fit with any work that he had done before but that seemed interesting. He set aside 30 minutes each day to read about something on his list. One thing led to another and Leon ended up in the same field, which wasn't planned, but in an entirely different position in a different department.

Reinvention often requires big change and some sacrifice on the front end to get to where you want to be. You will want to create a strong support system as you take steps to move forward with your reinvention. Rely on supportive friends, family, trusted coworkers, networking groups and organizations, teachers, and others to cheer you on and provide you with ideas and feedback.

Take Action

1. Have you considered a reinvention? Why or why not?

2. How could you build on your current knowledge-base and skills to reinvent your career? Make a list of at least ten of the skills that are key to your current or past position. Next, brainstorm ways that what you have done might fit with something that would interest you in the future. If you need help with this, discuss it with someone in your support network.

CHAPTER 16

Your Squad

We all have a squad. You might prefer to think of your squad as your council. Regardless of what you call it, they might have some great insights for you, if you just ask.

In Chapter 5, when we looked at *Whose Dream is it Anyway*, I cautioned you against working in a position that someone else nudged you into, unless the job is truly a good fit for you. This chapter might seem to be contradicting that advice, but it really doesn't. Your squad knows you better than anyone else and they are going to have insights that you should at least take a little time to listen to.

Picture yourself in a huddle with five to ten of the most influential people in your life. Maybe you have a parent, mentor, child, sibling, friend, co-worker, therapist, coach, uncle, or neighbor in your group. These are the people who you trust, who know you, who support you, who cheer you on! This is your squad. If you are having difficulties determining who might be on this list, return to the Chapter 5 *Take Action* questions that you answered. In Chapter 5, we looked at whether you are living your dream or a dream that belongs to someone else. Why might you look at the list that you created in Chapter 5? If someone has been able to influence you, they may be a member of your squad.

Bailey's squad included her mother, her past supervisor, two close friends, and her neighbor. These were her go-to people. They were honest with her and knew her well. She decided to ask her squad some questions to help her as she embarked on her career journey.

Bailey started by asking them about her three greatest strengths. She was surprised to learn that three of the five members of her squad thought that she was a natural salesperson. Bailey could talk a reluctant member of her squad into trying a new restaurant that he otherwise would have never visited. She could persuade her mother to take a vacation. She was a change agent with the ability to nudge others to help them embrace change. Bailey had never thought about this much, but she was good at helping others see possibilities. She didn't push them, but she would enthusiastically explain the benefits associated with one of their choices. She used this information to think about whether or not she had an interest in a sales position. While she didn't want to be in traditional sales, she thought about career possibilities that would involve a sales component.

Mark asked a friend to join him for an adult beverage after work. This was the same friend who Mark had worked with several years ago. They had maintained their friendship even after Mark left to work for another employer. In fact, they still played basketball at least once each month. Mark felt awkward about asking his friend for help as he contemplated a career change, but he needed to bounce his ideas off a trusted former colleague. By the end of their time together that evening, Mark's friend had solidified two of the ideas that Mark was considering as well as offering up a few ideas of his own. The after-work meeting ended up providing Mark with more valuable input than he had received from any other source.

Take Action

1. Who is on your squad? Make a list of those people. Start by listing anyone who comes to mind. After you have created your list, ask yourself these questions:

    a. Do I trust them completely?

    b. Do they support me unconditionally?

    c. Does this person act as my cheerleader?

    Edit your list accordingly.

2. Next, ask each member of your squad to list your three greatest strengths. Encourage them to be specific and to use more than one word to describe each one.

3. Take inventory. Do you see themes in the responses you received? Write about them.

    Bonus: If your squad member is up for it, take them to breakfast, lunch, coffee, or out for an adult beverage, and toss some ideas around.

CHAPTER 17

Tweaking What You Have Now

There are so many reasons why you might want to stay with your current employer. You may be in a situation where longevity with an organization entitles you to benefits that you would not likely find elsewhere. Retirement benefits, vacation time, and benefits associated with seniority may have lead you to think that you need to stay where you are. There are situations when insurance benefits may be even more important than the job itself. If you have decided, for whatever reason, that you need to stay where you are, but you are not happy in your current position, reinvent it.

Can you transfer to another position with your current employer? Sometimes a lateral move, or even a move that some might consider a demotion, just makes sense. You probably are aware of other positions as they become available. If you are not, contact your friendly human resource representative and find out how positions are posted and filled. Do internal candidates have first dibs?

Most of us would hesitate to accept a position that others would view as a demotion, but if you are unhappy in your current job and want to stay with your employer, a demotion might be a good option. You can learn something new or simply do something different. Research positions in your organization. Ask leaders for informational interviews where you have an opportunity to ask questions about a position. An informational interview is something that you can request from a potential employer or at your current place of employment. Request 15 to 20 minutes to visit with someone about a specific position or about an area of work. You should explain that you are gathering information as you contemplate a Career Yaw and that you understand that this is not a conventional interview for a position. If granted, come prepared with four or five thoughtful questions about the position and be ready to listen.

A note about demotions. A demotion is only a negative move if you view it that way. You can frame it however you wish. Some individuals are less concerned about this than others. If you need help framing this job CHOICE differently, seek out others who have made a similar job move. Consider working with a career coach or ask someone in marketing to help you explain your job shift if you feel the need to explain yourself. By the way, you don't.

Luna moved to another position in her organization that meant a lower rate of pay and a perceived lower status. She wanted to break into Information Technology (IT) but knew that she would need to start at the bottom in the department. So, she did. She accepted an entry level position, took a substantial cut in pay, and learned all she could about the department. She volunteered to take on tasks that others viewed as mundane and was soon recognized for her willingness to learn and her can-do attitude. Within two years, she had moved into a more advanced position and was making more than she had prior to her IT move. Plus, she has an entirely new marketable skillset. The best part is that Luna enjoys her work and looks forward to continued learning and promotion opportunities.

You can also look for training opportunities with your current employer without leaving the position you have now. Many employers now offer tuition reimbursement, or even pay for complete degree programs, through reputable universities. Use the benefits that are available to you to grow your body of knowledge and to advance your education. It may lead to a different position in your organization, or it may allow you to move to another employer in the future. Advancing your education may result in increased earnings. Research learning options that are available to you including certifications, seminars, undergraduate or graduate degrees, or on-the-job training. You can grow your knowledge base while you figure out what is next. As you learn, you will also discover what is most interesting to you.

If there are no other options available to you internally, then maybe it is time for a side gig. Is there a way that you can carve out a few hours each week to create your own learning opportunities or to take a part-time or volunteer position that will allow you to learn a new skill or to do something that you would enjoy? Oftentimes, what starts out as an interest turns into a passion and ends up being just the right creative outlet to complement what you have now.

Take Action

1. Make a list of all of the options that might be available to you at your current place of employment. Could you transfer to another department? Could you accept a lateral move, a demotion, or a promotion?

2. Is there something that you would like to learn more about that could help you in your current position? Is there something that you would like to learn that could help you in a future position?

3. Does your employer offer tuition reimbursement? Opportunities for internal training? Opportunities for external seminars or workshops? Research any learning opportunities that your employer offers. Gather the details and work your plan!

CHAPTER 18

Get Some Help Already

"I need help with this, but I can't afford it," is the most common objection to getting some career assistance that I hear. While I will be providing you with many FREE ways that you can get help if you are considering career options, I want you to think about why you should be considering professional assistance.

We are talking about your livelihood here. We are talking about a major part of your life. We are talking about your happiness. There are few areas in your life that are objectively more important than your career. Your family is more important. They may rely on you (or will rely on you) financially. Your health is more important. You will need the financial means to address health issues if they present themselves. Finances are tied directly to career.

Surely you can forgo that new electronic toy that will quickly be outdated, or that new piece of furniture, if it is the difference between you going it alone as you contemplate career options versus working with a true professional who is trained to help you. You are investing in your future and your happiness.

If you don't know how to find help, Google is your friend. Go ahead. Google career coaches. Ask your friends if they have ever used a professional career mentor. Read a few articles about career coaches. Contact your local higher education institution(s). There are so many options. If you test drive a career coach and you don't feel a connection or that there is benefit to you after the first session, move on. Finding the right coach is a little bit like finding the right car, or the right dentist, or a new friend. If you test drive it, have a cleaning, or have lunch together and something doesn't click, you move on. If the coach requires you to sign a contract prior to your first session or wants you to commit to something long-term before you have your first session, run!

And about that first session, most career coaches offer an introductory phone or video session lasting anywhere from 30 to 60 minutes. Many offer the first session at a reduced price. Test the water before you jump in.

Once you find the right coach, plan on a minimum of three sessions. Many will offer you a package. Expect to pay anywhere from $99 to more than $500 per session. It's an investment, but the returns are big.

Here are a few questions that you might ask a potential coach:

1. What are some of the tools you will use to help me?

2. Why should I work with YOU?

3. What are your credentials?

If you really cannot afford a career coach, consider less than conventional ways of paying for the coaching. Can you ask a family member to buy you a few sessions or contribute to a coaching fund in lieu of a more traditional birthday gift? Can you negotiate a pay-as-you-go contract with a coach where you pay for each individual session just prior to each session? If you live in the same area as the coach, can you barter for their services? (Talk to your accountant about this before you do it.)

You can also take advantage of many of the FREE career services that are available. While none of these will take the place of a great career coach, they can help you to move in the right direction. Here's a list to help you start to think about some of the resources that might be available to you.

- Ask a friend what they think your right work is. Better yet, ask five friends.

- Ask a parent or an older family member who knows you well what they think your right work is.

- Consider personality type testing and see how your results match those of other people who are living their callings. Does your employer or local community college offer personality type testing?

- Make a list of things that you are drawn to. Narrow the list by eliminating, one at a time, the items on the list that are of lesser interest to you until you are down to three. Then, share your list with someone you trust, or even half a dozen trusted people, and ask for their feedback.

- Take a class or start a book group focusing on finding your right work and explore the topic with others who are also searching.

- Contact the Career Services Center at your alma mater. Ask them what they offer graduates in the way of career assistance.

- Pick THREE things that you are committed to doing each week in the way of career exploration.

- Conduct informational interviews with people who are working in the industry or profession that interests you.

- Reach out to local universities and professional groups to see if they have speakers who focus on finding your right work or a related topic.

Another option is to consider an experience that immerses you in the career exploration process. You might attend a one-day seminar that helps participants to identify possible career paths. You might even think about attending a weekend retreat or similar exploration experience that offers you an opportunity to go all-in as you consider career options so you can be Happy at Work.

Take Action

1. What can you do today to bring you closer to your right work?

2. What can you do tomorrow, this week, next week, this month, and next month to make finding and moving toward your right work part of your everyday life?

3. Put action steps on your calendar.

4. Complete the action steps!

PART 3

Live It

CHAPTER 19

Whole Person

We all know someone who truly views their work as work only, more often, as a means to an end. Their job might be okay or even neutral on the love-it-or-leave-it scale. Usually the means-to-an-end person has made peace with this. Work is just work. They can compartmentalize work and separate it from other areas of their life. There isn't anything wrong with this. While it doesn't fit my personal criteria for work, it fits for them.

A few years ago, I worked with Cindy. She was neutral where her work was concerned. She worked in the sciences and her position fit with what she had studied in school. Her job didn't bring her joy or pain. It was just her job. It wasn't a placeholder. Sometimes we have a job for a predetermined amount of time while we finish school or before we know we are going to move to another state or country. This wasn't the case for Cindy. She had been doing her job for two decades and had no plans to leave her field or her employer.

Cindy's job afforded her everything she wanted financially and because she had two decades behind her doing the same work, she could get her work done in less than 40 hours each week. Her schedule worked well for her family and she spent her energy on interests outside of her office.

When Cindy left work at the end of the day, she moved from autopilot to superwoman. She was able to attend nearly all of her kid's school and sports activities. She had time to ride her bike, one of her true passions, for at least an hour every day. Cindy could afford fun vacations, live where she wanted to live, and be active in a variety of community volunteer groups. She loved what her work afforded her in her free time. Work was good enough and the rest of her life was wonderful.

**Each of us is a whole person and work is only
one part of who we are.**

It is easy to get so caught up in our job that we lose sight of the other pieces of our lives that are important to us. It is rare to hear someone complain that they play too much and just need to work more! It is more common to hear the exact opposite.

It can be difficult to gauge what is best for you as a whole person. This area deserves some extended thought if you haven't put time into contemplating who you are in the past few years. We lose track of time, balance, goals, interests, and who we are when we don't put time into rediscovery. At work we make plans. We create goals. We map things out for three years, ten years, or even a few decades. Plans change, but having plans and goals will help us to stay on track and live the lives that we are meant to live! Don't shortchange this process. Really *Take Action*!

Take Action

1. Consider your life in a big picture format. What are your priorities? List them in order. Look at all areas of your life. Consider home, leisure, community, and anything else that is important to you. After you have listed your priorities, rate them on a scale from one to ten.

2. Next, take your top ten and dig deeper. If number eight and nine on your list are gardening and attending your niece's

soccer games, it might be helpful to ask yourself the following questions. If I spent more time gardening and could only attend half of my niece's games, would I be okay with that? Then ask yourself the opposite. If knowing I could attend more than half of my niece's games but could rarely garden, would I be okay with that? Of course, you don't need to pick one or the other but going through this process with each item may surprise you! You may end up moving something higher or lower on your list of priorities.

3. Look at your list and think about your work and how it fits into the picture of you as a whole person. What does your work, aside from income, need to provide you with in each of the areas that you listed? Does your work provide you with what you need? If not, what can you do about it?

CHAPTER 20

Fall Into It

You might be one of the lucky ones. Sit with this for a few minutes. You might already know and you might already be doing what you should be doing. You might be doing your right work.

When I was a very young adult, I had a neighbor who was an optometrist. Sometimes I would babysit his children. Apparently, my uber-responsible approach to life caught his eye, and he asked me if I would like to work for him at one of his optical shops. I didn't know anything about the job but I said yes. I ended up working in the optical field off and on for about ten years. I became a licensed optician with self-study and by passing a comprehensive exam instead of attending classes. I enjoyed my time in the optical profession and am grateful for the opportunity that fell into my lap. For that time in my life, it was my right work.

Tara is in purchasing. She didn't set out to become a purchaser. It found her. She took a job as an assistant to someone in procurement and quickly found herself taking on more and more responsibility. Eventually, she took over her mentor's position. Today she is damn good at her job and she loves it! She has learned to successfully navigate the office politics (most of us have to learn to do this) and she decided this past year to go back to school to earn her bachelor's degree in her mid-forties so she can work her way into even more lucrative positions. She didn't decide to go after a job in purchasing. It found her. It is her right work.

Renada found her right work early in life. She loved little kids, even as a teen. She always thought that she would do something with children when she grew up. Renada became the most loved childcare provider in her neighborhood. When she started to contemplate careers, she knew that she wanted to work with preschool age children. She went to school to get her associate's degree in early childhood development and applied for positions with preschools in the metro area where she lived. She quickly landed a position and has been there ever since. Recently, she declined an offer to manage the facility. She decided that it would take her away from her true passion. She works as a mentor in her facility, but is clear that she doesn't want a fulltime leadership role. Not every day is a good day, but most of her workdays are rewarding and fun. The children love her! The parents love her too. She found her right work the first time and still feels the same enthusiasm as she prepares her room for the start of a new year as she did when she rode her bike to the neighbor's house after school to watch their two children.

My point is that sometimes people fall into the right position. Sometimes the job finds you. You might be doing your right work. If you are, but you feel like you need a boost, consider how you can take what you have and kick it up a notch.

Take Action

If you are already living your calling, what might you do to take it to another level? This is optional but worth your consideration.

1. Would you like to move into another position with your employer? What could you do to prepare yourself for the next move?

2. Is it time for you to take your talents and open your own business or partner with someone else who shares your same interest?

3. If you like what you are doing and don't want to move into another position or become an entrepreneur, how can you make your current work situation even better? Would another schedule help you to pursue other interests outside of work? Can you make your surroundings at work more pleasing? Is it time for you to mentor someone else?

CHAPTER 21

For Sure

There are some things that you know for sure. If you are like the rest of us, even though you know them for sure, you sometimes forget what you know, either purposefully or subconsciously. You know it but it might be convenient to forget it, or you might be so caught up in life, that it slips your mind. Take time to cultivate a list of what you know for sure.

What you know for sure can be something simple, like always setting your house to zero by picking things up, making sure that laundry is finished and put away, and having groceries on hand before Monday morning. You might know that doing those three things always makes your week better.

What you know for sure can be more complex. You might be a very compassionate person and want to help others but end up feeling depleted when there is nothing left for you. Rory struggles with this. He wrote, "I need to take care of me first. This always seems so selfish when I write it, but I know it is true. When I take care of myself, I have so much more to give others and my life is so much better."

One of my personal for sures is, "When I feel shortchanged by someone or something, I need to question my role in it, my thoughts, why I'm hanging on to it, what I can learn from it, and then let go."

When Wendy feels overwhelmed or limited by choices, she reminds herself that, "I am blessed with so many choices. I get to decide. What an incredible gift."

For sure statements can be about anything! They can include aspects of your spiritual life, things you know to be true for you around health and wellness, or lessons you have learned about finances. Other things you know for sure could be about your right work, preferences that you have regarding your environment, what you want less or more of, what makes you happy, a list of your priorities, what you have tried and know that you don't like, and things you have learned about yourself or your style. Your for sure list will likely need to be tweaked over time, but most of what you know for sure is likely to stick with you.

I like to read my for sure list at least monthly. Even though I've had a list for decades, I still need to be reminded of things that I thought I knew but forgot! These are lessons we teach ourselves and they can make our lives richer if we hang on to what fits for us. They can also help you with your Career Yaw. Reminding yourself of what you know for sure will likely lead you to your right work and solidify that you have found it.

What do you know for sure?

Take Action

1. Your for sure statements are unique to you! Start by writing down whatever comes to mind. You can refine your statements after you capture what you know for sure.

2. If you are having difficulty crafting your for sure statements, you can use these prompts.

   a. When I....

   b. I need....

    c. I like....

    d. I feel...

    e. Whenever I....

    f. Stop....

    g. I love....

    h. I don't want....

    i. I like....

    j. I want more....

    k. Spend more time....

    l. I gravitate toward....

    m. My preference is....

3. Read your for sure statements at least monthly. Consider updating them when you read them. If you wish, date them and watch how they might change over time and what stays the same.

CHAPTER 22

Sometimes We Like How it Sounds

What we do is part of who we are. Personal introductions often start with an explanation of what we do and, almost always, refer to our work. Ideally, what we do wouldn't be one of the first things that we tend to share in social situations. In fact, in some countries, occupation isn't shared until much later, if at all.

At times, we like to talk about our work but sometimes we don't. If we don't want to share what we do with others, we need to really think about why. Are we ashamed, embarrassed, afraid that they will charge us more for their services, or is it something else?

And if we like how it sounds, why? Is there a degree of prestige? Did your parents make a big deal out of what you do for a living? Is it important to your partner? Liking how it sounds can be a good thing. It might mean that we are aligned with our profession. It also might be a bad thing. It might mean that we are putting too much of what we do into who we are.

Sometimes when I work with large groups in a career coaching session, participants share their occupation, even if the instructions for introductions are vague and they are asked only to share five things about themselves. Although there are exceptions, it is often easy to tell which participants really identify with what they do. It is apparent that they like how it sounds. Some individuals are more neutral, and others are quick to talk about how they are looking for their right work. Keep in mind that the topic is career transition after all!

The type of position that someone has doesn't necessarily fit with whether the participant seems to like how it sounds. Someone can have what we might consider to be a very prestigious position and the person can seem to be very unimpressed with what they are sharing. Other times, the occupation might be one that most of the population would consider to be undesirable or mundane, yet there is a passion that is very apparent when they describe their profession.

Society is good at providing us with nudges about how we should feel about our work. Cultural ideas about what jobs are desirable and what we value may be very different. What is important is how YOU feel about the work that you do.

Sometimes we like how it sounds. Maybe we like it because we are proud of what we do or because we are perfectly aligned with our right work. Or perhaps we like it because it makes our mother happy.

This topic can be more complex than it might seem. Morgan liked their work as a professor at a state university, but for reasons that were not apparent even to Morgan, they didn't like telling other people about their profession. When we talked more about it, Morgan shared that their father frequently made comments about educated people who think they are "all that." Morgan was literally afraid of others labeling them as one of those people! Morgan decided to schedule a few sessions with a therapist to dig further into this. After all, Morgan liked their work and didn't want to do anything else. At the end of their a few sessions, Morgan found that they had worked through their issues. Even though Morgan generally is quick to share their enthusiasm around their work, Morgan also gives themself permission to use the label of teacher, rather than professor, when they are in a situation where they just do not want to share details. Afterwards, they are quick to move the conversation to another topic that is more comfortable for them.

Juan, a physician in family medicine, hated telling people about his occupation. He said, "Whenever I tell someone in a social situation what I do, they start sharing their medical problems with me. It is almost like I'm suddenly their private physician and they think it is okay to show me that thing on their arm at a neighborhood potluck." Over time, Juan learned to answer questions about his work another way. He says something like, "I'm a physician and I love my job. I try really hard to keep work at work and not let it bleed over into other areas of my life so I can continue to love my work. No one wants to be working all the time!" If you are hesitant about telling others about what you do, create your script and make it part of how you tell others about your work.

If you like how it sounds but you don't like what you are doing, it is time to review some of the other chapters in this book. You are not doing your right work. Contemplate some changes.

Take Action

1. When someone asks you what you do, what do you say? How does it make you feel? Why do you feel that way? Does it fit for you?

2. When someone asks you what you do, what would you like to say? If it isn't what you are saying now, how could you make it part of your narrative?

CHAPTER 23

Stacking

Hello COVID, my dear friend. I've come to talk to you again (if you are old enough, you can put a tune to this). COVID?! A friend?! Good things can come out of bad things.

Pre-COVID, our workplaces had a rigidity that, in most cases, wasn't to be questioned. You arrived at work at the start of your shift and you left to go home at the end. In some professions, this isn't very negotiable. I'd like to give a shout-out to our healthcare workers and all the other workers who don't have much in the way of flexibility because of their professions. Although, I would argue that a great employer would still provide you with some choice. Perhaps the employer could offer five eight-hour, four ten-hour, or three twelve-hour shifts. Due to COVID, many of us have experienced a change in our workplaces or hours. More and more people are working from home, enjoying schedules that might involve time in the office but allow for some flexibility. Employees are looking at a multitude of other work arrangements that would have been considered non-traditional before COVID, but that are becoming more mainstream now.

These changes afford workers many potential advantages. One of those is stacking positions. Because of increased flexibility, you might be able to use your two-hour lunch break from your regular full-time job to put some time on the clock for your part-time job during the day. This option might make it so you have other part-time options that you would not have been able to consider previously.

Merit is one of the most valuable employees at her full-time pace of employment. She works for politicians who rely on her incredible skillset and talents to make them shine. She is a legend in her industry. One of Merit's superpowers happened to be her ability to write grants. She was a grant-writing machine and used her skills to help a variety of non-profits that she supported. She donated her time and enjoyed making a difference. One of the non-profits asked her about a part-time gig. They wanted to hire her to help them on a more regular basis. She would be a part-time employee and they would compensate her handsomely for her work.

Merit checked with her full-time employer. (I always recommend this as full disclosure is the right thing to do!) Her manager considered the organization and other parameters of the offer and agreed that it would not cause a conflict. Merit took the part-time job in addition to her full-time work.

Merit is bringing home a bigger paycheck with her part-time job than she is with her full-time employer. She enjoys her full-time position, which includes full benefits that are important to her family, and Merit has no plans to leave either position anytime soon. She does, however, know that she has options. She could take on three part-time clients instead of having just one, and quit her full-time job. She could negotiate a part-time job with her full-time employer to free up time for more grant writing on the side. Or, she could stay just where she is at now, which is her plan, and enjoy the ride. The flexibility that her full-time position affords her makes it possible for Merit to schedule the occasional necessary meetings during the regular workday with her part-time client. Merit can take a longer lunch for a phone meeting or schedule an early morning meeting and start her workday at her full-time job at 10 a.m. on rare occasions. It works for both of Merit's employers.

Stacking positions can work. Merit stacks her part-time position on top of her full-time job. Some independent contractors stack several contracts with different employers. Other employees might work the required 30 hours for one employer in order to get full benefits and work 15 hours for another to learn a new trade. There is no right or wrong way to do this.

Changes in our workplaces have left us with options that might not have been available previously.

This is good stuff.

The gig economy is a buzz phrase that we hear often. What does it really mean? It can refer to workers who are stacking positions. It can also mean something else. Generally, the gig economy refers to individuals who take on short-term, flexible, or freelance jobs. This gives workers autonomy and choice that they might not have with traditional employment. It can benefit businesses too since they can bring on an expert or a temporary worker who takes care of their needs in the moment. Even though there are many benefits to the gig economy, relationships between employers and workers change when an employee is temporary. The worker has little in the way of assurances that they will have work next month, next week, or even tomorrow. Conversely, the employer often cannot rely on having workers when they need them. Another downside is that there are benefits and other perks that might be offered through an employer that are not available to gig workers. Finally, the gig worker is responsible for withholding and paying their own taxes.

Just recently, news about an employee who was working three full-time jobs hit my newsfeed. It seems that the employee was not an independent contractor and was truly working three jobs from home.

The employee admitted that the third job was just too much, but they were bringing in three salaries so they thought that they would at least try. Most employers have rules about what employees can and cannot do outside of work hours, and it is hard to believe that anyone could work three full-time jobs and experience a conflict of interest.

An independent contractor could work three full-time jobs without fear of repercussions if they did not have anything in their contract that prohibited them from doing so, but performance would likely suffer. This brings us to the idea of quiet quitting.

Quiet quitting is a relatively new concept. A quiet quitter is likely to do the bare minimum in their position. This may be a result of burnout, they may be actively looking for another job, or they may be working multiple jobs. The worker isn't actually quitting, at least not yet, but their work performance declines, which affects the organization.

Quiet quitting doesn't seem to be a very good long-term solution. You might consider other options first.

Take Action

1. Is stacking an option that might be available to you? Why or why not? Who would you need to talk to in your current position to find out?

2. How might you stack positions? What might you be able to do to learn something new or supplement your income? What might you enjoy doing? Why?

3. Are there reasons why you need to be employed as an employee of an organization? Are there reasons why you want to be an independent contractor?

CHAPTER 24

All the Other Stuff

How much fun is this? Seriously! Are you learning things about yourself that you already knew but had forgotten? Are you discovering things about yourself that you didn't know? What have you learned? How can it help you?

There is no right way when it comes to finding your right work but your Career Yaw can lead you to places that you may have never imagined. You can love your work. If you don't, make sure that you are clear about the trade-offs that you are making, and that you have peace with them, at least for the immediate future. Remember that your job should be one of your happy places, most of the time. We all have aspects of our employment that we don't enjoy even if we have found our perfect work.

There are several models for change. Research models for change and see what fits for you. If you want or need to make changes, spend some more time on the *Take Action* suggestions in this book. And if you have decided that you are where you need to be right now, give yourself permission to enjoy and even elevate your current work environment.

Take Action

1. When you reflect on the exercises that you have completed as you've read this book, which two or three stand out for you? Why? What were you reminded of or did you learn about yourself?

2. Where do you get stuck? What do you do to get unstuck? Do you have a plan?

3. Create a visual of your Career Yaw. Ask someone who you trust to look at it. Pay attention to how it makes you feel.

PARTING THOUGHTS

Yaw is a term that is used to describe an oscillation or a twist, often referring to a moving aircraft or a moving ship. It is a definitive movement off the charted course. In the context of this book, yaw refers to an oscillation or a twist off a charted career path. It is finding your right work and charting your own course. Your Career Yaw will be unique. Your path might be relatively straight, or it might look like an aerobatic airplane in the sky! My hope for you is that you enjoy the process, embrace the oscillating and twisting maneuvers, and find and acknowledge your right work. You can be Happy at Work and experience career movement with meaning.

Made in the USA
Las Vegas, NV
27 May 2023